Alcohol and Drug Interventions: Just the FAQ's

Introduction:

The faces change but the stories stay the same.

He said he'd cut back on his drinking.

She told you she stopped taking prescription pain pills that she didn't need.

His drinking has only become worse. That's why he lost his chance of a promotion at work and is about to lose his job for showing up drunk. He knows his liver is giving him problems, but that doesn't stop him from popping open another beer, unscrewing the top of a bottle of whiskey, or sitting at the local bar for hours on end and putting his and other people's lives in peril on the way home.

She's moved on to other drugs because the prescription pain pills don't have any more refills. Her boyfriend left her because drugs were more important to her than he was. She'll do anything for the next buzz or high - even if it means risking pregnancy, jail, or death.

Promises made. Promises broken.

This pattern continues to repeat as long as active addiction is in the picture. In fact, things will continue to get progressively worse unless some sort of intervention happens. That is the nature of addiction.

These two examples are far more common than we care to admit. As a matter of fact, the reason why you are reading this book probably has to do with a similar situation in your family or circle of friends. It's painful for you to watch your friend or family member destroy his life and impact the lives of those around him. It's simply heartbreaking to witness a person who was once full of happiness and joy now spiraled down into the depths of despair, loneliness, and maybe even death. You can't bear to watch as she drinks or drugs herself into oblivion. There is often a sense of helplessness that seems overwhelming.

There's a part of you that wants to do something to make them stop drinking or see to it that they never abuse drugs again. But there's also a part of you that's reluctant..... Scared. Terrified. That's the part that wonders if doing something, talking about what is going on would make matters worse.

To put it bluntly, doing nothing with regard to seeking help for your loved one's substance abuse problem. This, however, is the worst thing you can do. Doing nothing is going to allow things to get worse. That's what we call the "progressive nature of addiction" it will get worse without help.

The real question is how you can take action and get your loved one into rehab as soon as possible. Help can sometimes mean a local Alcoholics Anonymous or Narcotics anonymous meeting. Help can sometimes mean taking them to the hospital. Help can sometimes mean taking them to a drug and alcohol rehab. The best way to do that is to have an experienced drug and alcohol intervention specialist assist you in performing an intervention on your family member or friend who is suffering at the hands of addiction.

What's meant by an intervention? What do I need to know about the intervention process?

This book covers the three stages of alcohol/drug intervention:

1) pre-intervention;

2) intervention; and

3) post-intervention recovery.

Each stage has its own unique set of challenges and potential hazards. So, please don't take this book to be the "be-all and end-all" of information as it pertains to substance abuse intervention. The intent of this book is to provide a general overview of alcohol/drug interventions and the possible outcomes that might occur. It is not a substitute for a professional.

The specific results for your situation are dependent upon a wide variety of determining factors and circumstances. Of course, the goal of an intervention is to get the addict to treatment and transitioning into recovery. However, don't be surprised if the intervention and transition to recovery turns out to be turbulent at times. In fact, prepare for it, brace for a storm. It might not happen, but be ready if it does. But don't lose heart. Your interventionist will do his or her best to help the entire family through turbulent times. Helping a person into recovery from an addiction can be flat out messy at times. Knowing that you have done everything you can to help someone you care for who is struggling is relief of its own.

It is our sincere desire for you to gain a better understanding of what goes through the mind of the person abusing drugs or alcohol, gain the needed courage to intervene, and develop the patience for the addict after he transitions into recovery by taking it one day at a time.

A drug or alcohol intervention is a phone call away. For more information, go to alcoholdruginterventions.org. The time to intervene is now!

The National Addiction Recovery Alliance

October 26, 2011

Part I: Pre-Intervention Stage

How do we know it's time for an intervention?

When, exactly, is it the right time to perform an intervention on someone close to you who's tangled in the web of substance abuse? There is no hard and fast answer, but there are signs and symptoms that indicate that your loved one's drug and/or alcohol abuse has gone far enough.

Here's a list of common symptoms of substance abuse:

- *Little or no interest in activities they once enjoyed*
- *Telling you their substance abuse isn't really that bad*
- *A once pleasant attitude has morphed into paranoia, fear, and rage*
- *Impaired cognitive functioning*
- *Manipulating the truth to deny the severity or presence of an addiction*
- *Casting blame on others for their problems in life*
- *Anxiety, depression, feelings of worthlessness, paranoia, apathy, irritability*
- *Isolation, and withdrawing from people who care*
- *Little or no communication from the addict*
- *Escalating legal problems*
- *Missing work or school*

Keep in mind that this is not an all-inclusive list of the various symptoms of drug or alcohol addict will present. There are other symptoms not listed in this book, but these are often some of the most prevailing. Some symptoms are more obvious than others. Symptoms such as little or no interest in activities they once enjoyed are easy to spot. Deception, Lying, and negative emotions are more difficult to detect. If you notice any of these symptoms, your loved one needs help – and fast. Go to www.alcoholdruginterventions.org. Experienced intervention specialists stand ready to help you and your family.

The substance abuser, who has turned into an addict, might marginalize their addiction and the associated problems that they experience with drugs or alcohol, saying "It's really not all that bad. You are over-reacting. I have it under control." You may also notice, as is the case with an alcoholic, the smell of alcohol wafting from their pores. When people abuse drugs or alcohol long enough, their senses become dulled. They don't realize how strong the smell of alcohol is coming off of them, or they are in denial about the affects their drug use having on their life. When you try to lovingly point out problems, don't be surprised if your loved one abusing drugs or alcohol gets defensive. Unfortunately, that's normal for someone with a substance abuse problem. Does that mean you should keep your mouth shut when you smell drugs or alcohol on their breath or can see the pinhole retinas caused by heroin use? Absolutely not! Even though you might face stiff opposition, remember that the drugs and/or alcohol have a firm command of your loved one's life. You are not talking to the "real person".....you are talking to a person that is in the grips of an addiction. In that case, be prepared to hear some ugly things come out of the addict's mouth. They might say some to the effect of:

- You're a liar!
- You don't understand!

- You're out to get me!
- You don't know what you're talking about!
- Or let loose with a string of expletives
- You don't love me...

As hurtful as it is for you to hear those types of outbursts, try not to take those responses personally. That's easier said than done – to be sure.

You may also notice other different physical changes like bloodshot eyes, yellowing eyes, pinpoint pupils or a glazed absent person. Be aware of sudden changes in mood. An addict's mood can be quite volatile, or they can go into hiding. The temptation is there for the family to tread lightly around the addict in order to keep them from exploding in a substance-induced fit of rage or an emotional outburst on feels like the scale of a nuclear meltdown.

Sometimes you'll find that the addict is starting to lie more frequently in order to get away with his or her substance abuse. As far as lying goes, it starts off something simple such as saying, "No I wasn't drunk (or high) last night." For the addict, the lying and deception escalates to the point where they have to constantly become more creative to hide their addiction. Some people think it's a good idea for you to check for different places in the house where the addict stashes drugs or alcohol in a squirrel like fashion. You might find bottles of booze or plastic bags of drugs in the strangest places. That's why it's important for you and the rest of those who care about the addict to scour the house completely, leaving no nook or cranny unchecked. The reality is that addicts can be very creative with where they hide their means for getting drunk or high and while you might find and dispose of "the problem" temporarily, there will always be more until the underlying driving forces of the addiction are dealt with. In reality, drinking and drugging is but one symptom of addiction. That is why professional help and treatment is so important to make a lasting change.

For example, one alcoholic used to bring vodka into the house mixed in with a 32 oz. sports drink. This particular alcoholic knew exactly how much of the sports drink to consume before dumping in a 200 ml bottle of vodka. That way he could pass it off as a "sports drink" and go down into the basement so his wife and kids wouldn't know that he bought vodka when he wasn't supposed to. He then spent the afternoon drinking the sports drink, but it was half filled with vodka. That way he could "check out" for the day.

The preceding example is but one of many examples of how the lying and deception continues to increase until the addict thinks that they're hiding their addiction successfully from the rest of their family and friends. The addict doesn't realize you're onto him/her because in their drunken stupor or in their state of being high they think they're being clever. When, in fact, you know that there is a serious problem. And you want that problem go away. But the problem won't go away on its own. If something isn't done soon, a love one's drug or alcohol addiction will continues to spin out of control. Perhaps even to the point of death. Take a look at Amy Winehouse. Jeret Peterson. Elvis Presley. Janis Joplin. Jimi Hendrix. All those people died because someone didn't take it upon themselves to intervene in time. Granted, that's the worst-case scenario and some people reject treatment. But it's not a scenario that needs to happen in your life. You don't have to face the problem alone.

Why should we have an intervention specialist help in the first place?

This is a common question asked by many family members that we talk to. So, why exactly should you have a professional intervention specialist do the intervention as opposed to your pastor, priest, rabbi, or other spiritual leader? The answer is simple. Not many spiritual leaders are trained in the specifics of alcohol and drug interventions or drug and alcohol counseling. Clergy members have an understanding of the spiritual needs of the person and the family affected by drug and alcohol abuse, but they are not specifically trained to deal with the physical and emotional effects of drug and alcohol abuse. That's not to say that your rabbi, pastor, priest, or other spiritual leader can't be present at the intervention or can't assist with the intervention, but there are certain roles that have to be upheld during the intervention process. The best time for your spiritual leader to do his or her work is usually after the person has started into recovery and is feeling the spiritual void that chemicals had been filling. That's the appropriate time for any spiritual counseling to occur, when they are open to the spiritual message. .

Another question people often ask is why can't someone who is in Alcoholics Anonymous (AA) or Narcotics Anonymous (NA) facilitate the intervention? The answer to that question is not unlike the last, as it is the focus of the person who is performing the intervention. Although a person who has years of sobriety under their belt as a part of AA or NA, the focus of AA and NA is different than from an interventionist. Whereas with an intervention specialist the intervention specialist focuses specifically on the point of getting the addict into treatment for their addition. The intervention specialist will escort the addict to a treatment facility for the addict can get the medical care that he or she so desperately needs. Although a member of AA or NA might be able to relate to the pain of addiction, the odds of the person going to treatment are much higher here when an intervention specialist is present.

Valuable time and the effort can be wasted in trying to get the addict into treatment by not using a specialist in the field. It is worth the call to have a trained and experienced intervention specialist to come visit your loved one who is suffering from drug or alcohol abuse, and specifically and objectively work with the family in communicating to the addict how alcohol or drugs is destroying their life and affecting the lives of those around him or her. That's why it's a good idea to get in contact if an intervention specialist as soon as possible. An intervention specialist is just a few clicks away at www.alcoholdruginterventions.org.

Part II: Intervention Stage

What happens during an intervention?

First of all, not all interventions are the same. Each intervention has a unique set of circumstances that can change without notice. The previous section of this book contained a list of the common symptoms of addiction. Those symptoms are often a façade, as the real problem lies underneath.

Don't let such a sobering thought deter you from going forward with a drug or alcohol intervention. Denial, fear, and hostility from the addict underscore the need for an intervention. Breaking through those barriers and avoiding "another failed attempt" to help is what an intervention is all about!

In the days leading up to the intervention, take note of the addict's state of mind at various times of the day. You may notice certain behavioral patterns occurring at the same time of day. Take note of when the addict is "in a fog" from the lingering effects of a blackout or an ongoing high; or, you might find them to be agitated, angry, and upset.

You hope to get some sort of clue as to what might be the right time of day for an intervention to be more successful, and what kind of frame of mind the addict *might* be in. The truth is there is rarely the "perfect time" to do the intervention. It just needs to be done before it is too late.

When you finally intervene, make sure you have a game plan. Don't wing it. If you try to intervene without a plan, the likelihood of the addict going to treatment that day significantly decreases. Thinking out every possible scenario is what the professionals do.

Naturally, the first step in formulating a plan for a formal drug or alcohol intervention is to call a professional addiction interventionist who will help you develop a comprehensive plan toward a successful intervention. The day before the formal drug or alcohol intervention takes place, your intervention specialist will meet with you along with the rest of the family and friends close to the addict. There will be much education on the disease we call addiction. The interventionist will talk about some of the specific things that will happen before and after the intervention and up until the time when the interventionist escorts addict personally to treatment.

For example, your intervention specialist will discuss:

- who speaks and when
- how to articulate how the addict is hurting himself and everyone present, and phrase it in a non-combative manner
- how he/she will serve as an objective 3rd party
- the different types of treatment that are available
- what life can be like for the addict during the initial stages of recovery
- what life can be like for the family of the addict in the days, weeks, months following the intervention
- what he/she (the interventionist) will do to escort the addict to treatment

It's very important that you know your role in the intervention process. You have a very specific role to play in getting your loved one to a treatment facility. Keep in mind that it's not your job to direct the intervention when you have a professional. You're part of the band, not the band director. The intervention specialist is there to lead the way. If you chose not to employ a professional, one person will need to take the lead and responsibility for directing everyone involved.

The intervention leader is the one who is an objective third party who can speak to the addict and point out all of harm caused by the addict that he/she doesn't realize. Plus, the interventionist has the unique advantage of being able to enter the situation without any emotional attachment. Most people, however, have an emotional attachment to the person who is suffering from drug or alcohol abuse. So when it's your turn to speak, lovingly and firmly tell your loved one how they have hurt you in the past, and are how they are hurting their relationship with you.

Once the interventionist escorts the addict to treatment, what should we expect?

There are various different types of treatment available for people suffering from drug or alcohol addiction. For the best course of treatment for your loved one addicted to alcohol or drugs, the intervention specialist and the medical professionals working with your family can help determine which path to take. However, understand that there isn't always a clear-cut course of treatment for the addict and the results of such treatment can vary greatly.

Here are the most common forms of substance abuse treatment accompanied by a brief explanation.

Detoxification: The process in which the substances the addict abused - whether it's drugs or alcohol - are purged from their system. This can take a few days or up to weeks.

Inpatient Treatment Facility: This type of facility operates somewhat similar to a hospital in which you are put into a dorm- or hospital-like room for anywhere from a few weeks to a few months, depending upon the severity of the addiction or number of addictions.

Inpatient treatment facilities provide a well-structured schedule and environment. Patients receive medical care, group therapy, individual therapy, and the opportunity to begin the road to recovery by attending 12-step meetings like AA or NA. Educational sessions on proper nutrition, fitness, and finding a positive outlet for stress relief help provide a foundation for sober living after inpatient treatment.

Outpatient Treatment: The addict is allowed to live at home, but goes to the individual and group therapy sessions at a local clinic that treats addictive behavior. The duration and intensity of treatment will vary from place to place. Some outpatient programs consist of four, 4-hour sessions per week for up to 28 weeks. Other clinics offer four to five, 6-8 hour sessions for 4 weeks.

The therapy sessions and learning modules for outpatient treatment follow a similar schedule as inpatient programs, but in a longer drawn out process leaving many opportunities for relapse if a person is not highly motivated to change.

A four hour session, four times per week can be convenient for the recovering addict since he/she won't have to miss work or school as much. However, don't let convenience for your loved one factor in when determining the best course of treatment. Deep down, for some addicts, convenience – taking the easy way out of life's problems – was a driving force behind their drinking and using. Remember, your intervention specialist and attending mental health professionals can help you determine what's best for your loved one's situation.

Individual or Group Therapy: Finally, there's individual or therapy which is usually the last phase of transitioning from addiction into recovery. The type of individual or group therapy that's needed varies from situation to situation. There often needs to be ongoing individual therapy in which the recovering addict sees a certified alcohol and drug counselor from a couple of times a week or a couple of times a month.

Once the best course of treatment has been identified, (ideally by a professional trained in addiction assessment) stay committed to that particular course of treatment (unless, of course, the situation worsens). Without firm commitment on your part to help and encourage the addict through treatment, and without firm commitment on the part of the addict to complete each phase of treatment, relapse for the addict is just a drink or a hit away.

A note on the addict going solo toward recovery...

Sometimes addicts try to quit boozing and using on their own. This is sometimes called a white knuckling, cold turkey, or some other name that describes going on giving up drugs or alcohol on one's own. This type of recovery is not advised. Repeat after me, "Quitting cold turkey is **_NOT_** advised." Why? Because it is all the more easy for the addict to relapse and with certain drugs it can be fatal. Most people trying to quit alone fail because there is no accountability for the addict to check-in with a sponsor from Alcoholics Anonymous or Narcotics Anonymous. Not to mention the addict's body goes through a detox process to get rid of the alcohol or drugs in the person's system.

The side-effects can be too much to handle on one's own. In that case, it's better for the addict to be under the care of a licensed medical professional or certified drug and alcohol counselor.

Part Three: Post-Intervention and Recovery

What are some things I should be aware of when my loved one comes home from treatment?

The most common misperception people have about drug and alcohol addiction, especially those who are not afflicted by the disease, is that people think that the addict can be cured. An addict is never cured, but like diabetes, the addiction can be managed. Period. Whether it's an addiction to alcohol, cocaine, marijuana, heroin, methamphetamines, or any other illicit or prescription drug, he or she is never cured.

When the person is in recovery, you'll quickly find out that recovery from alcohol or drug addiction is a lifelong journey well worth taking. At times the process of recovery may seem the addict and all who are related to him or her are on a fishing boat in the Bering Sea during a wicked rain and windstorm. The waves of negative feelings, resentment, and despair crash over the side of the boat of recovery, causing it to pitch and roll violently. Other days will be peaceful and calm like a beautiful sunset witnessed from a tropical island. Granted, those are the physical, emotional, and psychological extremes associated with recovery from drug and alcohol abuse, but extreme times can, and do, occur for both the addict and the family.

After the intervention phase, in the post -intervention and recovery phase, you'll notice emotional, psychological, and physical changes in your loved one who is recovering from drug or alcohol addiction. Often communication channels once closed reopen at a new deeper more meaningful level.

Remember the comparison of the recovering addict feeling like he/she is on a fishing boat in the Bering Sea? You will notice that emotionally, at first, the addict will seem to be on that boat with waves of emotion buffeting him about. Be aware that some days are better than others. One day all is well in the world. Maybe even a few hours later their world comes crashing down once again.

The best thing to do is to be patient with your loved one who is who is recovering from drug and alcohol addiction; because their emotions will get the better of them some days.

You'll also notice psychological changes. Even though they might not realize it, drug and alcohol addicts have a "me first" attitude when boozing and using. By nature, alcohol and drug addiction are fueled by self-centered behavior. For example:

- How can *I* escape from *my* life and the world around *me*?
- What can *I* do to get more alcohol/drugs to make *me* feel better?
- It's not *my* fault I'm like this.
- *I* wouldn't be like this if you wouldn't be on *my* case all the time.

Sound familiar?

But now that he or she is in recovery, understand that he or she is doing his or her best not to be selfish or to have a self-centered attitude. That may not always seem to be the case. But, again, be patient and lead by example.

Other psychological changes you may notice in the recovering alcoholic or drug addict may include:

- A more positive outlook on life
- The "everybody-is-out-to-get-me" type of thinking is diminishing
- Irrational thinking is replaced by well-reasoned and responsible choices

Now that they've had the opportunity to go through treatment, things are starting to make sense to them in life. You'll begin to notice a more positive outlook from the person who's recovering from drug or alcohol addiction. You'll notice a little bit more of a bounce in their step as they won't be quite so lethargic. As a matter of fact, they might be fully alert to their surroundings.

Keep in mind also notice some similarities.

- Emotionally, as was said before, there will be down times days in which nothing seems to go right for the alcoholic or drug addict.

- Psychologically, there will still be an egocentric attitude and attitudes of being defensive, annoyed, or even downright nervous, but the delusional paranoia will be replace with a hope for a better future.

Keep them going and encourage them to keep going with their recovery program one day at a time. It is also important to take care of yourself.

Some people think that recovery is one thing that is that it is an event that takes place over a short period of time. That's false. Recovery takes place one day at a time…… for the rest of the alcoholic's or drug addict's life.

I feel like I still can't trust him or her and post-treatment is that normal?

Yes, it's normal not to trust your loved one who has been afflicted by drugs and now and alcohol. After all, they lied to you. How can you trust them when they did so many things to break your trust and to ruin the relationship they have with you? Words alone from the alcoholic or drug addict won't rebuild the bond of trust you once had. Over time, the addict's actions will have to prove that they are trustworthy once again.

However, trust and permission giving is a two-way street. Here's an example from one alcoholic:

My wife and I have been married for 12 years. For 7 of those years, I drank myself into oblivion. My wife pleaded with me to stop numerous times. That was until she laid down an ultimatum – I had to choose between her or the booze. I chose her. Five years after choosing her over the booze, I feel like she still doesn't trust me. It's almost as if she still sees me as the raging alcoholic I once was instead of the recovering alcoholic that I am and strive to be. I have no doubt the wounds run deep for her. After all, I broke the bond of trust between us by all the drinking I did and the consequences that followed – job loss, financial problems, anger issues, etc. Even though I can't undo the past and all the hurt I caused (although I wish I could), I can only try to shape the future by showing her I am doing my best to be the man she married, not the monster whose life was ruled by booze. Even though it must be painfully difficult for her, I wish my wife would exhibit some semblance of trust just like when we were first married. I guess I'll just have to keep showing her I'm trustworthy by letting my actions do all the talking.

This man's situation is not that uncommon. Husbands and wives, boyfriends and girlfriends, friends and life-partners who have been traumatized by a loved one's addiction often find they can't trust the recovering addict as they did in the past.

Think of it this way, since the trust between you and your loved one was broken, the way that trust is going to have to be restored through is similar to the same concept that President Ronald Reagan used on the Russians the agreement to reduce nuclear weapons was signed: ***Trust, but verify***.

I can drink in moderation and I don't do drugs. What should I do so my family member/friend doesn't relapse?

That's a great question. First of all, as a responsible person you have in mind the well-being of your friend or family member who has been afflicted by drug or alcohol abuse. That's great! That's why you've taken the time to assess the situation. Ask yourself if the party or function you attend is going to cause your loved one to relapse and fall off the deep end into alcohol and drug abuse? Is your going to this party, or that bar, or the social function the cause to get the ball rolling toward your loved one's relapse? Use your head. Use your best judgment. You know what you're capable of doing. And you also know what your loved one who suffers from addiction is not capable of doing. It's wise not to put your loved one in such a situation.

Also, be open with your family member who is addicted to alcohol or drugs. Ask him point-blank, "Will my drinking or taking necessary prescriptions possibly cause you to relapse?" Being upfront and being honest is the best way to get a handle on whether or not you should drink alcohol or even take prescription drugs around the recovering addict. Also ask if it's better for him/her if you completely refrain from drinking when they're around. Again, that's putting the well-being of your alcoholic friend or family member ahead of your own well-being and your own needs. That way there's less of a chance you'll have to handle unintended consequences later.

What should I do if or when he or she relapses?

For as much as we hate to think that relapse couldn't or wouldn't happen, it does. Many alcoholics and drug addicts relapse within the first few days, few weeks, or few months of going into recovery. As many as half of addicts will relapse within the first year of trying to get sober. Sadly, that's normal. But with that being the case, it's important for you to remember that it can be a learning lesson, or a fast track back into addiction insanity. It just depends on how it is handled.

As far as relapse goes, for you the concerned family member, you're best to be honest, and trust professional and 12 step help. It's hard. It's difficult. You're tempted to throw up your hands and give up. Please don't. Recovery can happen. But rarely does a person recover alone.

Should you need help when your friend or family member relapses into drinking or using, get in touch with the intervention specialist who helped your loved one seek treatment in the first place. At first, the intervention specialist can supply you with the verbal tools you need to help your loved one through the relapse. If necessary, the interventionist will come back and talk to the addict himself or herself in order to get the addict back on track for recovery.

If things are bad enough, don't hesitate to get the addict or alcoholic back into a treatment facility. For all you know, that relapse might be the last relapse. Honestly, that's not a good thing. Because that relapse just might kill them.

One option worth considering for trying to avoid relapse is for the recovering addict to enter a sober living house after being discharged from their initial treatment. For more information about sober living houses, our substance abuse professionals can help you. Simply go to www.alcoholdruginterventions.org for further details.

Final Thoughts

While portions of this ebook focus on the negative effects of addiction, that's not to say all is "doom and gloom" for the alcoholic or drug addict. There are many positive lessons and outcomes that can come from a drug or alcohol intervention. Who knows? Once the addict is in recovery, you'll have a better understanding of how addiction works from the perspective of the addict. Hopefully, you can have a renewed relationship with your father, mother, brother, sister, cousin, or friend that can be even better than before. You can take all you learned from the intervention, treatment, and recovery process and apply it toward helping a friend or a neighbor cope with the challenges they face with an alcoholic or drug addict in their family.

Of course, these positive outcomes don't magically come about. It takes time and effort to repair broken relationships and bonds of trust that have been destroyed. However, in the end, the time and effort for a positive outcome is worth it. No matter how long it takes. No matter the cost.

A drug or alcohol intervention is a phone call away. Experienced professional help is readily available to help you with:

- Organizing and carrying out a formal drug or alcohol intervention
- Finding suitable treatment options for your loved one
- Arrangements for your family member to live in a sober living house after going through rehab

For more information, go to www.alcoholdruginterventions.org. The time to intervene is now!

www.ingramcontent.com/pod-product-compliance
Lightning Source LLC
Chambersburg PA
CBHW070255290526
45789CB00004B/1869